Can We Talk?

The Art of Relationship Building

Rob Green

www.newgrowthpress.com

New Growth Press, Greensboro, NC 27404
www.newgrowthpress.com
Copyright © 2012 by Rob Green.

All rights reserved. No part of this publication may be reproduced, stored in a retrieval system, or transmitted in any form by any means, electronic, mechanical, photocopy, recording, or otherwise, without the prior permission of the publisher, except as provided by USA copyright law. Published 2012.

All Scripture quotations are from *The Holy Bible, English Standard Version®* (ESV®), copyright © 2000, 2001 by Crossway Bibles, a division of Good News Publishers. Used by permission. All rights reserved.

Cover Design: Tandem Creative, Tom Temple, tandemcreative.net
Typesetting: Lisa Parnell, lparnell.com

ISBN-13: 978-1-938267-91-8
ISBN-13: 978-1-938267-38-3 (eBook)

Library of Congress Cataloging-in-Publication Data
Green, Rob (Robert Eric)
 Can we talk? : the art of relationship building / Rob Green.
    p. cm.
 Includes bibliographical references and index.
 ISBN-13: 978-1-938267-91-8 (alk. paper)
 1. Conversation—Religious aspects—Christianity. 2. Interpersonal relations—Religious aspects—Christianity. I. Title.
 BV4597.53.C64G74   2012
 241'.672—dc23
                                                    2012026548
Printed in Canada

21 20 19 18 17 16 15 14   4 5 6 7 8

Bob turns out the lights on another day, a day just like yesterday. Home used to be where he wanted to be, but not anymore. In fact, Bob often works late or looks for an excuse to stop somewhere—anywhere— on the way home. Julie, his wife, feels exactly the same way. Bob and Julie are frustrated that they cannot talk about anything significant without the conversation sparking another argument. They argue about their children, their relationship, their money, and sometimes they just argue to argue. But this is not the way Bob and Julie want their relationship to be. They love each other; they want to spend meaningful time together; and they want to communicate well. But it seems that the more time they spend together and the more they talk, the worse their relationship becomes. They both feel trapped. They want to communicate well with one another, but they just don't know how.

You might be reading this minibook because Bob and Julie's story is like your own. You have challenges in your relationship, and you know it. Or perhaps your relationship is more peaceful than Bob and Julie's, but you would still like to grow in communicating well. Let me first say that you have already taken an important step. You should be encouraged that you recognize the challenge and are ready to take steps to improve your relationship. Second, your situation is not unique. You might feel like you are the only one with problems like this, but many people have similar struggles. You are not alone. Third, I want to encourage you that there is hope found in Jesus Christ. Your communication with others (or just your significant other!) may not accomplish the goal of connecting right now, but the good news is that it can radically change. There are many people like Bob and Julie whose relationships have been transformed because of what Jesus is doing in their lives. That can be true for you as well. Change starts with recognizing you have a problem and then asking God to help you. He will answer your cry for help.

Jesus came to save us from our sins, bring us into relationship with him, and help us in the midst of our sin and suffering. God has also given us his Word to direct our words and our lives. As you ask God, he will, through his Spirit, give you help to understand why you have so much trouble communicating and how to communicate in a way that builds up your relationships instead of tears them down.

Communication Begins with What You Want

Learning to communicate well is not just a matter of learning better, clearer ways of expressing yourself. Instead, you have to start where Jesus starts when he talks about your words—with what is going on inside of you. It starts with looking at *why* we say the things we do. Jesus says that it is "out of the abundance of the heart the mouth speaks" (Matthew 12:34). What does he mean by that? In the Bible the word *heart* is often used to describe our inner life—our thoughts and desires.

This is different than we usually think, isn't it? How often have you thought or said something like, "I didn't think before I spoke," or "That's not what I meant to say"? But Jesus is saying the opposite: he is saying that our main problem with our words is not that we speak without thinking, but that our words express what's in our hearts. In other words, our mouths say only what has already been thought. The path of communication is from the inside out. The starting place for all communication (both good and bad) is the heart. That is why it is not possible to make everything better simply through communication techniques. There are many couples (like Bob and Julie) who hear truths about communication, but don't improve their communication because no change has occurred in their wants or desires.

If you want to communicate so that your relationships are strengthened rather than torn apart, you will need to think biblically about your heart—the control center for all that we are and do.

Communication Expresses What You Want

Everyone's speech flows from what they want or desire in a certain situation or relationship. Think about it: when you argue with your spouse, aren't there things you want and aren't getting that are at work in that argument? When you speak kindly to your friend, but criticize your neighbor, aren't there desires motivating your words? James 4:1–2 explains it like this:

> What causes quarrels and what causes fights among you? Is it not this, that your passions are at war within you? You desire and do not have, so you murder. You covet and cannot obtain, so you fight and quarrel.

James says that our conflicts are not the result of a poor response from our spouse, their annoying tone or abrasive body language (even though all those things are wrong). Instead, conflicts come from our desires, the same desires that are waging war inside of us (v. 1, "is it not this . . . ?"). This truth is huge! It helps us understand something important—conflicts occur because we want certain things. Notice how the text explained it: "You desire . . . so you murder." There is the problem: you want what you want, and you do what it takes in order to have it. Obviously, if you want one thing and your spouse wants another, conflict is the inevitable result. Bob and Julie's desires resulted in communication (action), and the type of communication they used resulted in arguments, frustration, and anger (consequences).

No communication struggle can properly be addressed without first dealing with the heart. Thankfully, we have a Savior, Jesus, who has encouraged us to pray for help to change our desires so we will want to love God and love others. Let's return to Bob and Julie's struggle and examine the details of their situation to help us understand how what we want affects our communication.

What Bob Wants

We asked Bob to start thinking about which of his wants and desires lie buried underneath how he communicates with Julie. As he considered the way he communicates with Julie, certain desires began to stand out. First, Bob often wanted Julie to agree with him. Obviously, as a married couple, spouses want agreement a good percentage of the time, but Bob discovered that he *demands* agreement from Julie. If Julie simply wants them to "agree to disagree," Bob becomes upset and frustrated.

For example, Bob and Julie had planned to go on a date. With four small kids, alone time was a valued commodity. As the couple prepared for their date, Bob asked Julie if she was going to wear a coat. Julie replied that she was fine and explained that they would be indoors the majority of their date anyway. Bob could not believe his ears. He asked Julie, "Do you realize how cold it is?" When Julie responded that she was aware of the temperature, Bob further commented, "If you don't wear a coat, you might get sick." Bob thought that if Julie were to get sick, it could mean that his kids would get sick and he would have to take care of them alone! Bob thought Julie was being inconsiderate, and Julie (not being able to read Bob's mind) thought the whole discussion was silly.

Although the formal argument only lasted about ten minutes, Bob was irritated and Julie was exasperated for the rest of the evening. They continued their date, but this ten-minute argument created consequences that lasted the whole evening. Instead of having a wonderful time together, it became one more evening filled with irritation. Instead of building their relationship, it was another example of why their relationship so often feels like a struggle.

Bob's desire for Julie to agree that wearing a coat was a responsible and right thing to do lead to division, separation, and frustration. This illustration may seem trivial, but it is played out every day in marriages, in the workforce, and in parent-child relationships. In hindsight, Bob realized that the problem had nothing to do with the coat and everything to do with another self-centered desire of his—wanting not to take care of his children while his wife was sick. He was not interested in loving Julie sacrificially as God calls husbands to do (Ephesians 5:25). Instead, Bob was protecting himself at Julie's expense. Worse, he acted as if he were concerned for Julie's health when really his only concern was for how her choice might inconvenience him. His own hypocrisy blinded him to his sin and demonstrated the shallowness of his spirituality.

Do you see how the message of Jesus could have radically impacted Bob's motives? Isn't it possible that had he reflected on what would please the Lord (instead of what he wanted) and asked for the Spirit's help during this moment, things would have been radically different? Bob needed to understand that the conflict was not about a coat; it was about his relationship with the Lord Jesus and his unwillingness to love Julie sacrificially like Christ loves the church.

Bob also identified his desire of wanting problems to be solved quickly. In Bob's mind, Julie wanted to talk about the same problems again and again without doing anything differently. It drove him crazy. Bob thinks that the core of insanity is doing the same things over again while expecting different results. Not only did Bob think these conversations were crazy, he was not interested in spending forty-five minutes discussing issues he considered trivial. Bob's desires directed his behavior. He was short tempered. He did not pay close attention to Julie and often did not look at her when she was speaking. Why? Bob wanted the thirty-second version of the four problems for the day, and then he wanted to be done. Once again, Bob was really about Bob. He was not thinking about Jesus, the gospel, or praying for the fruit of the Spirit to be present in these moments. He was not interested in helping Julie; he was interested in helping himself.

Do you see how some simple desires of Bob's heart have created an environment of tension and frustration? Can you see how very small issues (like a coat) become large issues and place a couple in a position where everyday conversation is difficult? Can you see that without a change in Bob's heart these same desires will continue to result in strife and division? The point is that people's desires determine the words they use, the tone of their voice, their attentiveness in conversation, and their body language. Unless Bob refocuses his self-centered desires on Jesus, asks him for mercy to love others more than he loves himself, and asks him for help to turn from what he wants and instead consider what's best for his spouse, the communication problems will remain. On the other hand, Bob and Julie's date night could have been radically redeemed if Bob's heart had been fixed on pleasing Jesus. Since communication failures are rarely a one-way street, let's turn our attention to Julie's desires.

What Julie Wants

As Julie evaluated their marriage, she realized that one of her major desires was to be heard. From

Can We Talk?

Julie's perspective, Bob did not seem to care about her opinion. It seemed to Julie that Bob wanted to give an answer to a problem and move on to something else. Julie felt like Bob regularly ignored her. As a result, she reacted in frustration. Sometimes she cried to get Bob to look at her long enough for her to speak a few sentences. At other times she fought back in anger. And sometimes she stopped communicating altogether.

At one level, Julie can be applauded. She is trying to connect with Bob. She wants to engage him and talk things through. However, when Julie's desire to be heard becomes the most important thing to her, her communication becomes negative. When Julie does not find her security in Christ, her relationship with Bob is impacted. When Bob's approval (instead of her desire to please Christ) becomes the most important thing in her life, then that desire rules her inner life and affects how she talks to Bob. Inevitably, she does not want to serve Bob, but to punish him through anger and resentment.

Also, when Bob gives Julie an opportunity to talk, Julie wants Bob's undivided attention. The key word is *undivided*. When Bob tries to multitask while Julie talks to him—by going through the mail, cleaning up the kitchen, or reading the paper—she goes ballistic! Suddenly the living room is turned into a small-scale version of Mount St. Helens. Julie demands his undivided attention. She can't believe how insensitive and uncaring her husband is. Once again, Julie is not totally wrong. Bob is being rude and insensitive. Julie should lovingly confront Bob about his treatment of her. However, when she allows her desire for Bob's undivided attention to become more important to her than loving him, then living out of God's love has taken second place in her heart to getting what she wants from Bob and punishing him if he doesn't do as she demands.

The Scriptures teach that how we talk reveals something we want deep down inside us. Our words are an outflow of something that is present on the inside. It is here that Bob and Julie need to focus. For their communication to improve, what they want has to change. They have to want to know and love Jesus more than they want to agree, to solve problems quickly, to be listened to, and to have each other's attention. They need to desire to please God with their responses. They need to repent and turn away from these desires that have become too important and turn to Jesus.

After they identified their desires, a wonderful thing happened in Bob and Julie's life. For the first time they realized why they had the same old arguments. They realized that there were things they wanted on the inside that were appearing in ugly ways on the outside. What they wanted from each other was not wrong, but they realized that wanting anything more than loving God and each other was wrong. Once they saw what they needed forgiveness for, they could go to Jesus for forgiveness and help. In this case, Bob prayed and asked God to forgive him for wanting to be agreed with and wanting to be efficient in problem solving *more than* he wanted to honor Jesus and love his wife. He asked Julie to forgive him for not loving her like Jesus loves the church. He committed himself to pleasing Christ above those other things. Julie asked God and Bob to forgive her for wanting to be heard and wanting Bob's undivided attention *more than* she wanted to please Jesus and love her husband. Bob and Julie's communication struggles were not solved overnight, but these insights filled them with hope.

Use Bob and Julie's experience to help you think about what desires you might have made more important in your life than pleasing Jesus. Answer the following questions as a way to identify those desires and turn to Jesus for help.

1. What are the issues you most commonly argue about with your spouse (or even your child or a coworker)? (for example, finances, care of children)

    a.

    b.

    c.

    d.

2. What are the most common desires you have when discussing the issues you listed above? (for example, to have my opinion clearly heard)

    a.

    b.

c.

d.

Jesus Wants Heart Change

Done? Great! Congratulations. You are learning truths that many of Jesus' hearers never understood. They were so busy worrying about behavior that they completely missed the issue of examining the motivation behind their actions.

My guess is that some of the desires you listed are not automatically sinful. Instead, they are like Bob's or Julie's. You want to be heard, agreed with, paid attention to, and be a problem solver. But just like Bob and Julie, you also notice that it is not the desire itself that is sinful; it is the importance of the desire. A good desire becomes a sinful desire when it rules and controls your heart. Your heart is made to worship only one thing at a time. You can't worship Jesus and still put what you want first. It just won't work. That is why passages like 2 Corinthians 5:9 and 1 Corinthians 10:31 explain that pleasing Christ is our most important priority.

How can you want to please Christ more? Start by remembering his kindness and mercy to you. Think back to the time when you first trusted Christ. He forgave you, removed your sin as far as the east is from the west, and gave you security for eternal life in heaven. Is it possible that you have lost sight of your love for him? If so, turn back to him and ask him to forgive you and renew you so that you can love him with all of your heart (Matthew 22:37–38). Start your day by reminding yourself of what Christ has done for you. Spend time meditating on the grace of Jesus. Think about God's lovingkindness to you and your family. Search through the Psalms and underline all the phrases that describe what God has done for you. Write a list of all the things Jesus has forgiven you for. Spend time thinking about his sacrifice for you on the cross. Who else deserves first place in all our desires and affections? It is the past, present, and future work of Jesus that should motivate you to love him and find joy in him.

When you seek after God, you find him. When you beg him to help you grow in your love for him, and then he increases that love. Communication struggles start with the heart and so does communication redemption. Your sinful desires have already brought you heartache. Desire the Lord and you, like the psalmist, will "taste and see that the Lord is good!" (Psalm 34:8). "Delight yourself in the Lord, and he will give you the desires of your heart" (Psalm 37:4).

Jesus said in John 10:10–11, "I came that they may have life and have it abundantly. I am the good shepherd. The good shepherd lays down his life for the sheep." Abundant life! Jesus did not say he would help you tolerate life, slog through life, or survive life. He said he would give you abundant life! How could it be any other way? Jesus is *the* good shepherd, *your* good shepherd. The transforming power of the gospel not only changes your eternal destiny, it also impacts the words you say today.

Take a moment to review your list of desires. I encourage you to repent of any wrong desires and of anything that you have made more important than pleasing God. Repentance means to turn in a new direction. By going to Jesus for forgiveness, you can turn from self-centered desires that hinder your communication and turn toward Christ, who will change you to be like him. Only the Spirit can give you what you need to build up your relationship—desires that are God–centered. Resolve to make pleasing Christ your top priority. The Lord has made you his own and, according to Romans 8:31–39, has freely given you all things. There is nothing you lack. As you turn to him, Jesus can change your desires so that your words are characterized by love for God and love for one another.

Jesus Wants to Change Your Communication

How does Jesus change our desire life? It happens as we turn away from our self-centered desires and reflect on all that Christ has done and is doing. As we grow in our love for him and as our desires become focused on doing what pleases him because we love him, the way we communicate changes. Since our heart is the source of all we do and say, when our heart loves Jesus, it is natural that loving actions follow. God calls all who are saved to live out God's Word in practical ways. Ephesians 2:8–9 talks about our salvation, and then verse 10 explains a loving response to our salvation: "For we are his workmanship, created in Christ Jesus for good works, which God prepared beforehand, that we should walk in them." For those who love Jesus, this is not drudgery (although it certainly is a struggle). Instead it is a privilege and a joy.

You might think, *I am growing in my love for Jesus. I know my communication always flows from the inside out, but what about some practical tools. Does the Bible give any of those?* The answer is an overwhelming *yes*. Over the years in our counseling ministry, thousands have been helped by some practical communication principles outlined in the Bible.[1] Below are our principles that will give you specific direction on living out your love for Jesus in the way you communicate with others.

Four Communication Principles

The Bible has a lot to say about communication, and just one minibook cannot capture all of it. However, one of the best texts for you to read about communication is Ephesians 4:25–32. In order to understand this passage it is important to consider the context. In Ephesians 4:17–24, Paul explains that when you trust Christ as your Lord and Savior there is a radical change of thinking and behaving. You are a new person in Christ and in union with him. You have the Holy Spirit in you, so you can live as an ambassador for Jesus. God changes your heart; now it is time to live a changed life. Paul explains that a believer should not act like an unbeliever, but rather should be exchanging sinful patterns for godly patterns. This process of becoming like Christ (progressive sanctification) is made possible as our minds are renewed (see also Romans 12:1–2) and transformed by the grace of God.

When you put James 4:1–2 and Ephesians 4:17–24 together, you see that everything we put in the center of our life that is not Christ needs to be put off. Instead, a new way of thinking and behaving must be put in place. In Ephesians 4, Paul explains several new ways of thinking and behaving and most of them have some relationship to communication.

Truth 1: Be Honest

> Therefore, having put away falsehood, let each one of you speak the truth with his neighbor, for we are members one of another. (Ephesians 4:25)

At first glance honesty seems so simple. Yet all too often our communication contains various forms of deceit. For example, (1) lying no matter how small or "innocent" the lie might be; (2) using body language and words that do not seem to match; (3) exaggerating and not letting our audience know that we are exaggerating; or (4) using absolute words like *never* or *always*. In the fourth example, our communication does not accurately represent the facts. Instead, our words are used to tell another person how good we are or how lousy they are. The truth is your boss is not *always* mean, your spouse is not *always* insensitive, and your coworker is not *always* rude.

While honesty is not easy, especially in the midst of a conversation that is emotionally charged, verse 25 explains that we need to be honest because "we are members one of another." Because you are members of one another, you should not have falsehood in your communication. You cannot build meaningful relationships with others unless you are willing to be honest even when it is hard. The Bible says that wounds from a friend are faithful (but they are still wounds), and they are much better than kisses from an enemy. In a marriage, sometimes communication looks like a kiss from an enemy rather than a wound from a person who deeply loves you.

That was true of Bob. He focused on Julie's lack of concern for him (for example, not wearing a coat and getting ill as result) and then communicated dishonestly. If he had been willing to say from the beginning that he was concerned for his health and the family's health, he might have chosen to say nothing at all or at least could have expressed his concern in a loving manner. His lack of honest communication made the problem worse.

After Bob and Julie began to focus more on their love for Jesus and finding joy in their relationship with him, they began to communicate honestly. They worked hard at expressing the "real" issue instead of hiding behind a false idea. As a result, they could trust what the other was saying and they could talk about the real issues in their lives. What are some of the real issues that you are not expressing in your closest relationships? Some of those you should express to your spouse. Even if you have uncovered that the real problem is your self-centeredness, you can still share that with your spouse and ask for prayer that you will change. Your honest communication, expressed wisely, will build your relationship instead of tear it down.

Truth 2: Keep Current

> Be angry and do not sin; do not let the sun go down on your anger, and give no opportunity to the devil. (Ephesians 4:26–27)

Couples often struggle to solve today's problems today. Problems seem to go unresolved, or the conversation that attempts to resolve problems ends up creating more problems. Unresolved problems often lead to bitterness (Hebrews 12:15). Bitterness is evidenced when a problem is brought up again and again to criticize and condemn. Over time, the bitterness associated with unresolved problems grows large enough that no meaningful relationship is possible until the bitterness is faced and removed. Instead of solving today's problems today, individuals are forced to deal with a lot of past baggage. But, as the saying goes, "problems are like bunnies, you can have two today or one thousand tomorrow." This is just another way of saying that it is important to deal with the problems before they multiply.

Bob and Julie struggled here as well. Their pattern of focusing on their own desires instead of pleasing Christ was habitual. Thus, they were both exceedingly bitter regarding the other's failures. It was easy for them to argue because they were already looking for selfishness in the other person. Bob should have regularly pursued his wife, not avoided her to keep the peace. Julie should have forgiven him for not loving her well, not held a grudge and lashed out when she couldn't take it anymore.

As Bob and Julie learned to put this rule into practice, they gradually discovered that the only thing they had to overcome was today's issue. There was no more "remember fourteen years ago when . . . " or adding old issues to new ones. Instead, Bob and Julie simply focused on the current problems and rarely lived with unresolved conflict.

Truth 3: Attack the Problem, Not the Person

> Let no corrupting talk come out of your mouths, but only such as is good for building up, as fits the occasion, that it may give grace to those who hear. (Ephesians 4:29)

Another common communication problem occurs when one person attacks another, rather than attempting to deal with the problem at hand. Not focusing on the problem often results in repeated personal attacks that hurt the relationship and create new problems through hurtful speech. By attacking one another, you add trouble to the original problem. Ephesians 4:29 tells us this behavior is opposite to what God intends for our communication. Our words should be a conduit for grace, not a means of conflict.

Julie's eruption and Bob's insistence that Julie do what he wanted are classic illustrations of attacking a person instead of a problem. Once again, their heart's desires made it easy for them to attack. Their relationship history demonstrated a culture of attacking to win. Bob and Julie needed to remember that every time they used words to hurt and control one another, they abused God's gift of communication. In due time, they saw how much their communication hurt their relationship and grieved their Savior. Just imagine how different their evening could have gone if they had thought about communicating with words that gave grace. What if they had used their words to build each other up that evening, as Jesus would have wanted? Bob and Julie's evening could have been all that they had hoped and a breath of fresh air in the midst of a relationship that still had challenges.

As Bob and Julie changed, so did the amount of encouragement they gave each other. They worked to say things that would build up the other person. By using their words for encouragement they had less time to use harmful and destructive words. Bob and Julie began experiencing the blessings associated with loving Jesus and loving one another.

Truth 4: Act, Don't React

> Let all bitterness and wrath and anger and clamor and slander be put away from you, along with all malice. Be kind to one another, tenderhearted, forgiving one another, as God in Christ forgave you. (Ephesians 4:31–32)

While there is much to discuss in verses 31–32, there are two points that stand out. First, there are certain responses (actions) that should always be part of the way we communicate—words that express gentleness, forgiveness, and kindness. Would those who work with you describe your communication in these terms? Would your spouse? How about your children?

Second, the passage explains that there are certain kinds of communication (reactions) that are sinful and need to be stopped—words that express malice, clamor, and slander. Why? Because these things do not please the Lord. Are you quick to point out others' faults? Do you use a harsh tone? Do you assume the worst of people and then share your thoughts with others so that they will think the worst about people as well?

Once again, Bob and Julie clearly violated this truth. Instead of responding with gentleness, their interaction became increasingly intense. Usually, the longer the conversation lasted, the quicker the response from the other person. Their self-centered desires ultimately resulted in neither of them being able to follow any of the truths found in Ephesians 4:25–32.

The end of verse 32 provided something wonderful for Bob and Julie—a way to deal with the times when they reverted back to their old patterns. Bob and Julie were not perfect; they were taking steps of growth. Whenever they fell, there was the path of forgiveness—the same path they experience in their relationship with Jesus. They could stop and ask God to forgive them for their hurtful communication. Then, knowing their amazing forgiveness for Jesus' sake, they could forgive one another.

Thankfully, in the case of Bob and Julie, they began to see how their desires impacted their communication. They were willing to repent of self-centeredness and focus on the grace of Jesus. They focused on prayer and the Spirit's work. They memorized these communication truths and gently held one another accountable.

By God's grace Bob and Julie were changing. That same change is available to you.

Relationship Building for Life

It should be clear that changing your desires and your actions will take time, effort, and energy. The results, however, are well worth it! Just as you have experienced the negative impact on your relationships from self-centered desires and communication, you can experience results from godly desires and godly communication. Your ability to build and strengthen relationships whether in the home, the workplace, or local church will significantly increase as you turn to Christ for the help you need to live for him. Paul tells us in 2 Corinthians that when we are controlled by the love of Christ (instead of our own self-centered desires), we no longer live for ourselves, but to please Jesus.

> For the love of Christ controls us, because we have concluded this: that one has died for all, therefore all have died; and he died for all, that those who live might no longer live for themselves but for him who for their sake died and was raised. (2 Corinthians 5:14–15)

When you aim to please Christ, his Spirit will help you to build others up with your communication. As you do that, your relationships will become characterized by honesty, kindness, grace, and forgiveness. Below is a brief homework assignment that will help you get started. May God help you establish godly relationships as you trust him.

Application Questions

1. After going through the whole minibook, review your answers to the two questions found on pages 12–13. You may need to revise the answers you gave previously.

2. Keep a journal this week listing (a) the time and date of any arguments, (b) the main cause of the arguments, (c) your desires in the midst of the arguments, and (d) the results of the arguments. This exercise will help you deal with your desires, the principal point of the minibook.

3. Memorize the four principles of communication.

4. Identify which of the four principles you have the hardest time living out. Ask your spouse (or a friend you trust) to tell you if they notice you not keeping the rule you identified. Ask them to gently and lovingly discuss these instances with you.

5. Describe three or four instances this week where God helped you apply biblical rules of communication instead of following your old habits. Thank God for helping you change in this way.

Endnotes

1. Jay Adams may have been the first to list these truths in this way. At Faith Biblical Counseling, we have used them for years because they are so practical and memorable.